RECRUIT, HIRE, & RETAIN SUPERSTAR PART-TIME EMPLOYEES

Little Known Ways Small Businesses Can Find, Employ, and Keep More Qualified, Competent, Motivated People
By
Don Kermath

Copyright © 2023

www.DonKermath.com

Dedication

To my partner Becca, who left breadcrumbs for me to find her after 35 years apart. I'm forever grateful for a second life that includes you. I'm also grateful for the forensic and honest review of this book. You helped me see what I am uniquely unqualified to see about my work.

To the experts and mentors who helped shape and mold me. I wish I had heeded more of your advice.

To Leslie Westfall, Manuela Eldridge, and Michelle Norvell, all small business owners grateful for what they learned reviewing this book. I am grateful for your comments, ideas, and time which added value to this book.

Introduction

Why Hiring Wrong Is an Expensive Problem for You

Read this book if you want to avoid the pain and minimize the expense of recruiting, hiring, and retaining superstar part-time employees in a small business.

Hiring a new employee **costs an average of $4,129** (Northon, 2016) **to $7,645** (Glassdoor Team, 2019). For example, the 2019 U.S. Bureau of Labor Statistics (U.S. Bureau of Labor Statistics, 2020) estimates an annualized employee **turnover rate of 45.00%** across all industries. If you operate an 11-person staff, a 45.00% turnover rate will **cost you between $20,645 to $38,225 each year**.

There are solutions, and they're a lot easier than you might think.

This book is for the small business owner and manager who is fed up with hiring crappy part-time employees, tired of wasting time and money on those same slackers, and would like to get a handle on retaining their superstars. The ideas are sometimes radical, but always practical, tested, and easy to implement.

These ideas can never be used in large organizations—too many rules and too much control given to the human resources department. The number one complaint I hear from friends in large organizations is that they cannot get rid of whining, unproductive, toxic employees fast enough.

This book is going to suggest you bend, and even break, some of the traditional thinking around recruiting, hiring, and retaining part-time employees.

If it is true that you should fire fast, then it is in the small business arena where that kind of advice can be followed.

Author's Origin Story

"You've got to be crazy." That's what I said to my business partner and now ex-wife 25 years ago when she suggested we open an indoor tanning salon. "Don't you know the sun is bad for you?" I explained.

At the time we had a handful of employees running a professional commercial janitorial business. I was a US Army researcher by day and janitor some nights and weekends. **Neither of us knew anything about retail or indoor tanning**.

After extensive research trying to prove my hypothesis—she's crazy, I discovered the truth. **I was crazy for my irrational fear of the sun.** I learned you need sunshine like you need food, air, and water. I learned sunburn, not sunshine, was the real danger and easily avoided in the controlled environment of a professional indoor tanning salon.

Along the way, we learned marketing, finance, operations, human resources, and much more about running small businesses of many types. I received invitations to speak at conventions, consult small business owners, and conduct employee training.

Has anyone ever said to you, **"You should write a book."**? More times than I can count. Two decades later here is that book.

May this be the first of many. I've enjoyed the process and can't wait to start another.

I hope you make and save tons of money from the advice you find here.

೧೮

Don Kermath is the employee turnover reduction expert that empowers small business owners and managers to transform their workforce into productive, cohesive, team-players who stay for the long haul and contribute to innovation and excellence on the job (and could really benefit your bottom line).

Table of Contents

Dedication 3
Introduction 5
Table of Contents 9
Legal Notes 11
Chapter 1. Summary 13
Chapter 2. Include This Phrase in Every Job Posting 19
Chapter 3. The 3-Minute Superstar Screening Interview 29
Chapter 4. Getting Honest Answers to the Right Interview Questions 35
Chapter 5. Let Them Go in 5 Days 47
Chapter 6. Onboarding That Gets Employees Productive Quickly 55
Chapter 7. Deliver Smart Evaluations That Make Superstars Want to Stay 63
Chapter 8. Engaging Employees with Meaningful and Diverse Work 67
Chapter 9. Retire Demotivating Policies So Your Superstars Can Excel 69
Chapter 10. What's Next? 77
References 81
About the Author 83

Legal Notes

In my words…

I'm not an attorney, accountant, or plumber—do not construe any advice here to be legal, financial, or plumbing in nature. My successes and failures are my own. You might succeed or fail epically. **Hopefully, you'll learn from my failures to avoid your own**, but that is out of my control. You are the chef in your kitchen.

In an attorney's words…

Although the author and publisher have made every effort to ensure that the information in this book was correct at press time, the author and publisher do not assume and hereby disclaim any liability to any party for any loss, damage, or disruption caused by errors or omissions, whether such errors or omissions result from negligence, accident, or any other cause.

Copyright © 2020 Don Kermath All Rights Reserved.

Cover design with Canva.com by Don Kermath

Editing by Rebecca Hollinger

Small Business Owner Book Reviews by Leslie Westfall of Party Razzi Entertainment, Manuela Eldridge of SunCatchers Tanning & Boutique, and Michelle Norvell of Bare Necessities Tanning Salon.

Chapter 1. Summary

Spoiler Alert—Skip This Chapter if You Plan to Read the Entire Book

A book writing consultant told me **50% of the people who buy my book won't even read it**. That made me just a little sad.

And a handful of people, he said, will eat every word, digest it, and get to work doing what needs to be done. They'll pick and choose what will work for them, modify it, plan out implementation, and do it! They'll be the ones who end up immediately getting results saving money, saving time, and avoiding the headaches of recruiting, hiring, and retaining part-time employees. If this describes you, I recommend skipping right to the next chapter—I don't want you getting bored with the "to the point" nature of a summary.

Then the consultant told me there is a third and very special kind of person who will purchase your book—the skimmer, the person who would like to just have the "CliffsNotes©" version of your book. For the skimmer, he said to put a summary at the end of every chapter, which I did, because skimmers will read only the summary and call it done.

I'm guessing if that is you it's because you are too overwhelmed by day-to-day firefighting to invest the time and energy needed to work on your business instead of in your business. I've been there—done that—didn't like it—figured out how to reverse the narrative.

For those who don't have time or are simply incredulous that you will learn anything here, I give you this Summary. Read this chapter and call it a day. No reason to ruin a good binding on a book by making you go to the end of every chapter to find the summaries.

Chapter 2. Small Businesses Should Include This Phrase in Every Job Posting

No whiners. No lazy people. Nobody with too many "personal commitments."

To have a successful recruiting program you need to advertise **what you don't want** as well as what you do. Becoming a preferred employer means you don't have to work as hard recruiting and retaining part-time employees. **Preferred employers are not jerks** and they **fix broken promises quickly**.

While most small businesses offer competitive pay and benefits, you can excel by providing something few businesses do—**recognition** to your staff and theirs. All of this is not only a recipe for **fruitful recruiting but also success in retaining part-time superstar employees.**

Chapter 3. Saving Time & Money with the Three-Minute Superstar Screening Interview

Use this three-minute screening interview to prequalify whether you have a slacker or a potential superstar. There is no reason to waste your time on someone who does not meet your minimum qualifications. Or worse, if hired, will ruin your reputation, and drive your superstars away. You'll drastically reduce the number of slackers and people with too many personal obligations who make it to the formal interview process and into your workforce. **This will save you time, money, and headache later.**

Chapter 4. Getting Honest Answers to the Right Interview Questions

Hire for attitude and communicate anything you think might be untasteful but is a necessary part of getting your job done. The former is for your benefit and the latter is so the candidate can bail early before either of you have spent time, money, and energy in a working relationship.

Chapter 5. Let Them Go in Five Days

Set the unworthy new hires free in five days and everyone will be glad you did.

You'll drastically reduce the number of whiners, slackers, and people with too many personal obligations in your workforce. This will save you time, money, and headache later.

Chapter 6. Onboarding That Gets New Part-Time Employees Productive Quickly

You must determine what information to communicate during the onboarding: industry-specific, company values, and operational tactics. New hires should know how to use the tools of your trade, dress code, scheduling, payday, and all the other specifics. **Productive onboarding means your new hire stays**

for the long haul, understands your expectations, and is ready to hit the proverbial ground running—fast.

Chapter 7. Deliver Effective Evaluations That Make Employees Want to Stay

Forget the annual evaluations. Use a million micro evaluations all year long, both praising and reprimand varieties, to get the most out of your people so they can perform like superstars. **Your part-time staff will stay for the long haul because you've paid them lavishly in praise and recognition.**

Chapter 8. Engaging Employees With Meaningful and Diverse Work

Engage your employees by giving them meaningful and diverse work. You don't like doing boring things and you sure as hell don't want to do the same thing day in and day out. That's why I work for myself—meaningful and diverse work. Have them try your job or part of it. Cross-train positions—they'll be excited to learn something new and, wait for it, you'll have a backup for that position.

Go walk in your employee's shoes and if you are bored to tears, mix it up a bit for them.

Chapter 9. Retire Demotivating Policies So Your Employees Can Excel Again

Today, not tomorrow, analyze your existing policies for demotivating potential. 48% of your policies have the potential to demotivate. When you seek you shall find bad policies. Retire or change them before they cost you more money and talent.

While you are conducting this company self-awareness analysis, get your team together to figure out what your core values are. Once you have consensus, codify those values into a Code of Honor that gets the whole team playing with the same set of rules to create harmony. **Your superstars will stay for the long haul and be productive again which will improve your bottom line.**

Chapter 10. What's Next?

Use this three-minute screening interview in conjunction with accurate interviews, short probationary periods, productive onboarding, effective evaluations, meaningful & diverse work, and common-sense policies to recruit, hire, and retain superstar employees. You'll drastically reduce the number of slackers and people with too many personal obligations who make it to the interview process and into your workforce. This will save you time, money, and headache later.

If this sounds daunting, book a free consult with me to transform your workforce into productive, cohesive, team-players who stay for the long haul, and contribute to innovation and excellence on the job (and could really benefit your bottom line).

Chapter 2. Include This Phrase in Every Job Posting

So Your Superstars Don't Have to Put Up with Whiners and Slackers

Have you heard that job advertisements should not describe the position but describe the person you are looking for? In the same light, your adverts should also **describe what you don't want**. I learned this from the marketing Wizard of Ads, Roy Williams. We include this one phrase in all our job advertisements:

No whiners. No lazy people. Nobody with too many "personal commitments."

Figure 1. Social Media Post

I know, you are concerned about offending someone. Who will you offend? Whiners? Lazy people? People with too many "personal obligations?"

Example Job Listing:

Entry Level Opportunity of a Lifetime: *Are you dependable and resourceful? Are you out-going and dedicated? Can you sell and delegate? Would you like to work in a fun environment where you are expected to act and behave like an owner? Do you have lots of energy, intuition, and initiative? Do you present yourself well, and have computer skills?*

No whiners. No lazy people. Nobody with too many personal commitments.

Does this describe you? Email your resume. If you like, stop in any of our award-winning salons to talk with a manager or even an owner to get more details about the position.

Do you want them to waste your time, money, and energy? What if they make it through your interview process (because they are clever and know all the right answers to your clever questions) and mix with your workforce? **Do your superstar employees want to work with them?**

In 32 years of recruiting, hiring, and retaining employees, not always successfully, only in the last dozen years has it been necessary to maintain a constant state of recruiting.

Consequently, we've learned to **hire all superstars that come across our path**.

If you haven't figured it out by now you will. The most important resource is people—competent, qualified, motivated people if you can find them. So, when a superstar appears you make a place on the bus, as author Jim Collins says in his book *Good to Great* (Collins, 2001).

This is not as difficult as you might think. True, a small business does not have the financial resources to carry extra staff. Given the high employee turnover rates across all industries, especially among part-time staff, you can just put off the new hire by two weeks while you figure out how to make room on your bus.

To clear a space on the bus, ask yourself this question about everyone in your employ: "**Would I hire this person if they came in today looking for a job?**" If no, set that employee free. You'll both be grateful.

If you have no one to set free, congratulations, you have ample bench strength. Bench strength means you don't have that excuse for not setting free pigs in your employ. **Pigs are the employees who destroy your reputation and cause your superstars to flee for less toxic pastures.**

Pro Tip: *Did you know more people are killed by pigs than sharks? More businesses are killed by the pigs they hire than by the shark competitors trying to steal market share. Avoid or set free the pigs and the sharks become irrelevant.*

Mind blown!

To maximize your recruiting advertising dollars all you need to do is become a preferred employer. This is much easier than you think and here's why. Big business has a corporate office in some far-off city in a different state. You are a small business in your community, often where you've raised your family.

We have found building our community reputation and in turn, recognizing excellence in the community when we find it, are two keys to the perpetual flow of superstars wanting to work for you.

Here's how it works.

Community Reputation Means Don't Be an Asshole

There were several years when we frequently got nurses interviewing for positions with us. Turns out the doctors they worked for had a community reputation of being assholes. During the interviews, it took all my internal strength not to vocalize what I was thinking— "I'm so sorry you work for those assholes."

How do you build a great community reputation?

First, don't be an asshole.

How do you know if you're an asshole?

I like the attempt to quantify assholeness by Jeremy Sherman (Sherman, 2018) Ph.D., in his article Universal Qualities of Jerks. In a nutshell, assholes use their asshole powers to acquire more asshole power all the time, pretending it's for the greater good.

Here are a few of Dr. Sherman's traits of the absolute butthead:

"***Feigned invincibility***: *I win always.*
Reality is my slave: *Since I'm the most realistic, I've earned the power to control reality.*
Self-winding movement: *If you're with me, it proves I'm right. If you're against me, it proves I'm right.*
Pious nihilism: *The truth is that nothing is true. That means I don't have to fuss over what's true.*
Spotting spots on you proves I'm spotless: *So long as I can keep attention on your failings, I never ever have to consider the possibility that I'm wrong.*
Exceptional exemptionism: *I'm different from other people. I'm therefore exempt from the rules of society."*

It may be possible and is often true that assholes achieve greatness. Go ahead and achieve greatness, just know behind your back people are apologizing to your staff, "**I'm so sorry you work for that asshole.**"

Second, do your level best to **quickly clean up and make right any customer service issues**. No one is perfect and no one expects you to be. But when you are wrong, admit it and fix it—fast. Oh yeah, **don't forget that your employees are customers too**—internal customers.

Here is our recipe for correcting our screw-ups:

Listen with empathy (take notes). I'm constantly amazed at how many upset guests calm down and feel relieved just to have someone listen to them. They only need to vent—they ask for nothing.

Repeat the issue back to the guest as you now understand it (this shows you are empathetic and demonstrates that you understand the real issue).

Apologize and explain that it won't happen again (make sure it doesn't happen again through policy and training if necessary).

Ask the guest what you can do to fix the issue (do not assume you know what the guest wants).

If it is reasonable, and it usually is, implement the fix. If it is unreasonable, offer a reasonable solution. You don't want to go bankrupt, but you also don't want a bad online review. (We are often able to give the guest an entire refund for a service or product they used but were unsatisfied with, for example, if they are willing to take the refund in the form of store credit.)

Many managers and business owners dread dealing with a complaint or unsatisfied customer. **I look forward to the opportunity to right a wrong—win back a customer lost.** Statistically, 80% of your clients will continue to do business with you if you properly and quickly handle your screw up. I like those odds.

Recognizing Excellence in the Community

Some of you are going to have heartburn with this suggestion. **We gently poach superstars from other businesses.** For many years I refused to engage in this recruitment strategy because I found it distasteful, unethical, and downright playing dirty.

Until…

I like to think we prepare our part-time staff to be excellent employees no matter where they end up after working for us. And that is apparently true because other businesses like to try and poach our employees. After a few too many successfully poached employees I began to justify playing the same game, but with a twist.

Pro Tip: We do not rehire an employee who leaves us for another job—especially if the reason is solely for more pay.

Around the holidays, the shopping mall stores try to poach employees from local businesses. They don't always pay more but they make promises of more hours and a permanent position if they like you. The problem is the mall stores never end up offering more hours or a permanent position and they layoff all the seasonal staff by mid-January.

As sure as cold weather in winter the prodigal ex-employee comes with hat in hand for their job back. All is forgiven, but you don't get your job back—it has already been filled.

*Unless you move out of state or quit for other reasons unrelated to your dissatisfaction with working for us, we don't rehire. We've made many exceptions to this policy and have **regretted it 100% of the time**.*

Your call.

We decided if other businesses were going to try and poach our staff with promises of more money, we would start trying to **poach their employees with something more valuable—recognition**.

We have a **Care-Bear award** we give to staff who exhibit exceptional customer care. We thought, why don't we give Care-Bear awards to employees of other businesses who give us exceptional customer care.

Here's how it works:

Carry a trinket (e.g., a small teddy bear) or a mini-award certificate printed on the back of your business card when you shop at local businesses.

Figure 2. Example Back of Business Card Care Bear Award

When you experience excellent customer care recognize the employee and give them the trinket or mini-certificate. Explain that this is what we do for our staff. We do not offer them a job. It's not necessary.

First, you'll be amazed at how good you feel when the **employee's face lights up with gratitude**. Second, be prepared for the following possible reactions: they might be speechless, their eyes well up, ask if you are hiring, give you even better service.

Our best employees are our best customers—we call them guests. We invite guests to join our team through in-store, text, and email marketing.

Our second-best employees were someone else's best employees—some call that poaching, I call it setting them free to pursue a job that is more rewarding and suited to their skills and temperament.

To have a successful recruiting program you need to advertise **what you don't want** as well as what you do. Becoming a preferred employer means you don't have to work as hard recruiting and retaining part-time employees. **Preferred employers are not jerks** and they **fix broken promises quickly**.

While most small businesses offer competitive pay and benefits, you can excel by providing something few businesses do—**recognition** to your staff and theirs. All of this is not only a recipe for **fruitful recruiting but also success in retaining part-time superstar employees**.

What's Next?

- ✓ Job postings must describe the person, not the position, both what you want and don't want. Include this line in every job posting to filter out what you don't want: **No whiners. No lazy people. Nobody with too many "personal commitments."**
- ✓ Evaluate your existing staff against these criteria so you know where to make room on your bus for a superstar: **"Would I hire this person if they walked through the door today?"**

- ✓ Become a preferred employer so superstars come knocking on your door.
    - o **Don't be an asshole!** Assholes repel potential superstars and chase away existing superstars.
    - o **Gently poach superstars** in your community by giving them something more valuable than money and in short supply—**recognition**.
    - o **Fix broken promises quickly**. No one is perfect and no one expects you to be. When you screw up, admit it, apologize, and make it right—fast!

Chapter 3. The 3-Minute Superstar Screening Interview

Why Interviewing Should Be Like Speed Dating

It's time to reconsider the traditional **hire slow and fire quick philosophy**—at least the hire slow part. Maybe hiring should be more like speed dating. Put many candidates across the table from you but spend little time evaluating them. You'll drastically reduce the number of clever slackers who make it into your workforce while **spending much less time and money**.

> **Pro Tip:** Once you determine the applicant meets the minimum job requirements, either from their application or resume, **give them an unscheduled call**.
>
> It seems like no one answers their phone these days; leave a clear, short message with a short deadline to call back. For example, "This is Jane from XYZ Company. Based on your application you look exactly like the superstars we hire. Give me a call by Friday so you and I can **clarify a few minor**

> ***points*** *before scheduling a formal interview."*
>
> *You've now just boosted their excitement level about your position and simultaneously calmed them down about a telephone interview—which is exactly what clarifying a few minor points is. Of course, leave your phone number.*

Once you have the applicant on the phone, take just three minutes to ask these screening questions. If they pass the screening questions, immediately schedule an interview for a later date. **A negative response to any of your questions disqualifies the candidate** for hire—end the interview. On a clean sheet of paper make notes as to why you disqualified the applicant, initial, date, and store your notes with the application in a reject folder.

> ***Consult your attorney for legal advice****: Prevailing advice on the interweb is to not alter an applicant's resume or application—don't even attach a sticky note and certainly don't staple anything to a resume or employment application.*

Move on to the next applicant. **This is speed dating, remember?**

The 3-Minute Telephone Screening Interview

1. **Do you object to a background check?** If you hire people with criminal records, give them a chance to come clean. Check their criminal record ahead of the call. If you don't have a service to check for you, search online for the circuit clerk in the county the candidate resides. Most records are online these days. In their answer, you are looking for remorse about criminal activity and honesty about having a criminal record. **One of my best employees was an ex-felon**.

2. **Do you have a valid driver's license and reliable transportation?** Clarify that transportation is available all the time, and in good working order. Oh, the number of times I've heard, "My car isn't working," or "My license is suspended," or other excuses an employee can't get to work. In these days of Uber, there should be no excuse for not getting to work—on time. Nonetheless, **we don't hire you unless you have reliable transportation for your personal use and a valid driver's license**.

3. **Are there any days of the week you cannot work?** We let part-time applicants slide on this because they are usually students or have other regular obligations. Full-time applicants must be available to work when our customers expect us to be open. It's hard enough to work around the schedules of part-time employees, you don't want to have to manage the variable schedules of your full-time staff too. **You may have a different opinion; it's up to you on this one**.

4. **Can you work Saturday and Sunday?** I know, we just asked if they are available 7 days a week, but somehow people still think that doesn't include the weekends. If you are open on weekends, best to ask and see if there is hesitation or backpedaling. Sometimes they'll ask, "Do I have to work every

weekend?" **That's an indication you'll have more problems than not getting them to pick up a weekend shift.**

5. Do you know any reason that could cause you to be late for work? First, you are telling the candidate **you expect them to show up on time**. Second, you are trying to uncover problems with getting to work, other obligations, or patterns of absenteeism.

6. If you hire students: **Are you involved in athletics, drama, music, or other after-school activities?** Do not hire any student involved in after-school activities. They'll tell you, last minute, "I have a mandatory meeting/event/game/practice so I can't come to work." Save yourself the headache, **don't hire students involved in after-school activities**.

7. Will you have another job if you work with us? Are you planning to make us your priority? We don't hire if the applicant has another job. One hundred percent of the time there is a scheduling conflict. If you are willing to deal with the frequent scheduling conflicts, determine if the applicant only wants your job to fill in around their other job. If so, they are disqualified.

8. What are your professional goals for the next 6 months? You are looking for professional goals that indicate the candidate might not be working for you in 6 to 12 months, like becoming a stylist, nurse, or emergency medical technician.

When you apply for a home mortgage loan the bank will prequalify you to determine if you can borrow and how much you can borrow. You'll have to answer a series of prequalifying questions, a 'screening interview' if you will. If you're a deadbeat and an excessive credit risk the bank will immediately tell you to take a hike. If you are a credit superstar then the bank falls all over itself to get you in to fill out the more complicated and involved loan application, the 'formal interview' if we continue with this analogy.

In the same way, use this three-minute screening interview to prequalify whether you have a slacker or a potential superstar. There is no reason to waste your time on someone who does not meet your minimum qualifications. Or worse, if hired, will ruin your reputation, and drive your superstars away. You'll drastically reduce the number of slackers and people with too many personal obligations who make it to the formal interview process and into your workforce. **This will save you time, money, and headache later.**

What's Next?

- ✓ **Hire fast and fire quick**—hiring part-time employees should be more like speed dating.
- ✓ Pre-qualify part-time employee candidates with a **three-minute telephone interview** to drastically reduce the number of slackers and people with too many personal obligations who make it to the formal interview process and into your workforce.

Chapter 4. Getting Honest Answers to the Right Interview Questions

Why a Formal Interview Is Almost Unnecessary for Hiring Part-Time Employees

Yes, I said it. A formal interview is almost unnecessary for hiring part-time employees. We hire nearly 90% of the part-time staff who make it through the *three-Minute Telephone Screening Interview* from the previous chapter **and** show up for the formal interview. Sadly, it's true; many candidates don't even bother to show up for a scheduled formal interview.

Do I need to say it? Don't hire them if they don't show up for a scheduled formal interview!

Why Is a Formal Interview Almost Unnecessary?

First, you've already asked and gotten the answer to the most pressing question most small businesses need to answer before hiring part-time staff: **Are you available when I need you?**

You'll likely be able to teach them everything about the position. Hell, I've even hired a bookkeeper with zero bookkeeping skills or training. There are so many online tools and tutorials for just about every skill you need to know. I don't even have to know the skill I need my part-time employee to learn.

What Is the Purpose of a Formal Interview for Your Part-Time Candidate?

You are looking to answer the one question you can't train.
What is their attitude?
You know this, I'm telling you nothing new.

You meet people every day. I bet you can form an opinion about a person's attitude within the first 30 to 90 seconds of meeting them. Am I right?

If you've done the *three-Minute Telephone Screening Interview,* (and I hope you have) then you've already spent twice as much time as you need assessing their attitude.

We use the formal interview for these three purposes:

1. Can the candidate show up on time?
2. Is the candidate willing and able to clean?
3. Is the candidate rude or polite?

Can the candidate show up on time?

Quite simply, did the candidate show up five minutes before the interview, right on time, after the scheduled appointed time, or not at all?

Pro Tip: *Five minutes early is on time, on time is late, and late is set free (or not hired in this case).*

Workplace tardiness and absenteeism have become endemic in the United States. I blame the big-box stores for being complicit in this societal disease. Big-box stores have such difficulty getting staff to even show up for shifts that they overstaff by up to 50%. You, on the other hand, have a small business to run and cannot afford to be so frivolous with your business expenses.

By the way, if you're wondering why you are having issues finding part-time staff it's also because of the big-box stores. This overstaffing management style is sucking up all the available resources because they are unwilling or incompetent to manage employee tardiness and absenteeism properly.

This might sound like a personal rant, and it is, but there is a larger point. If your applicant has a big-box store on their resume (or they put it on your employment application) you can believe that **they expect timeliness and showing up for a scheduled shift to be optional**. Buyer beware.

Finally, I wish it didn't need to be said, but if the applicant does not show up to the interview—**don't hire them!** No matter how desperate you are, and you are desperate if you are going after a candidate who didn't even bother to reschedule or cancel, don't do it. It's like the guy who doesn't get that she's just not into him. It's very unattractive.

Is the candidate willing and able to clean?

We've made it clear through our recruiting and marketing material how important cleaning is to our business model. We clean all the time, seriously. Our staff is expected to, on occasion, clean and sanitize toilets with a toilet brush, equipment with a toothbrush, and even floor-tile grout with a grout brush.

Between every guest, they are required to sanitize the room the guest used, and every hour sanitize all the surfaces a guest may have touched throughout the lobby and restrooms. During the formal interview, we want to make it clear—you are going to be cleaning.

If you have something like cleaning that might be untasteful but is an important part of the position, now is the time to be upfront with the candidate. Best to know now before either of you invest time, money, and energy into a working relationship.

Is the candidate rude or polite?

If being unwilling and unable to clean is our first unforgivable sin, then being rude would be the second. We will terminate your ass faster than you can say, "Bob's your uncle" for being rude to our guests or your fellow employees. Since we can't teach attitude, we need to know right here, right now, if the candidate is rude or polite.

We emphasize how important cleaning is so the candidate can walk away. We zero in on attitude so we can decide to walk away.

Determining a candidate's attitude is our main purpose for a formal interview.

Now, you might be thinking, "Why don't you just use a personality test?" We have. And you know what, they don't work for us, and here's why.

First, we are a small business with small budgets. Personality tests cost businesses real money—about $500 million a year (Meiner, 2015).

> **Pro Tip:** *100% of any expense you can cut (minus taxes) goes straight in the business owner's pocket. Let me repeat that; if you save $100 on a business expense, $100 minus income tax goes right into your wallet.*
>
> *Conversely, if you are operating on a generous 15% profit margin, then 15 cents, minus taxes, of every dollar your business makes finds its way into your change jar. So, make $100 and buy two over-priced lattes with your $15.* **Save $100 and you can buy an espresso machine to make your fancy lattes** *(yes, yes, yes, minus taxes).*
>
> *"A penny saved is a penny got." Old Ben Franklin was a genius.*

Second, the personality tests are wrought with biases (internal and external) and dissimulation (i.e., fraud). These tests are mostly introspective (i.e., subjective) self-reporting questionnaires.

Let me ask you a question. **Are you fully self-aware?** Can you look at another person without introjecting your prejudices? Do you know how to answer a question to elicit the response you think is most desirable? If you are honest you answered, no, I'm not fully self-aware, no, I have a lifetime of learned prejudices, and yes, I know how to fake the answer to a question.

There you have it. Personality "tests" are extremely subjective, inaccurate, and dare I say it, a waste of time and money for small businesses hiring part-time employees.

What we have learned is that active listening during all communications with the candidate is the best way to determine their attitude, especially rudeness versus politeness.

Don't forget to "listen" with your eyes too. Facial expressions can indicate emotion, intentions, and social goals according to psychologist Carlos Crivelli (Myers, 2018). Rolling eyes may be an indication of disrespect. If you have teenagers or have ever been one you know all the disrespectful facial expressions.

Here are some specific things to listen for:

1. Does the candidate **say please, thank you, and you're welcome**? I believe we expect kids to learn this by the third grade, but if they haven't then you won't be able to teach them now. I know, easy right? I never said this stuff was rocket science.
2. Does the candidate respond to a yes or no question with **"Yes/No sir"** or **"Yes/No ma'am?"** I call this southern hospitality or military respect. It doesn't mean they are not polite if they don't use this response, but it's a good indicator they are polite and respectful if they respond this way.
3. How does the candidate talk about life experiences, other people, and past jobs? You are looking for positivity. Do they focus on what they learned or what they lost? **Do they talk trash** or are they respectful, even if they were in a bad breakup or got fired? **Positive people are polite people**.

Pro Tip: Check out the candidate's social media postings before scheduling the interview. Look for trash talk, disrespectful *behavior, and negativity. These are all traits of rude people.*

In the end, it almost doesn't matter what you ask them as long as you let them do 90% of the talking and you are listening 100% of the time—eyes and ears.

Even though I believe the only wrong questions are the ones that keep your attorney up at night, I know you want specific examples related to part-time hires so here's a baker's dozen:

Reiteration of Legal Disclaimer: *I am not an attorney or a plumber, this is not legal advice, you should not consider this advice without consulting your attorney. And fix your own damn toilet.*

---

1. **What made you apply for this position?** This is the first warmup question designed to relax the candidate and learn something about your company's perception in the community. This data is pure gold. Also, I have found nervousness can negatively impact the candidate's true self from appearing. Give them time to loosen up.
2. **How did you hear about this job opening?** This is warmup question number two and designed to relax the candidate and figure out if our recruiting budget is money well spent.
3. **Briefly, would you summarize your work history?** I'm looking for two things here: first, will the candidate trash talk a previous employer, and second, have they worked for someone (like a big box store or a competitor) that

might have corrupted their work ethic. We've found retraining someone who has worked in a big box store or for a competitor is more challenging and may not be worth the time, money, and energy. We might not disqualify a candidate for this past work history, but if we must choose between two otherwise equal candidates, we'll take the virgin. I hope you understand virgin is a metaphor for the employee with no big box or competitor work experience.

4. **How do you feel about taking "no" for an answer?** We sell stuff in our business and all our employees are expected to sell, even part-time staff. I'm guessing your business sells stuff (service or product) too. If the candidate does not understand that "no" is just a prelude to "yes" then they might get an attitude when perceiving "no" as a personal rejection. If hearing "no" is personal, then they're not likely to be happy working for us—or anyone for that matter.

5. **How much supervision have you typically received in your previous job?** We do not micromanage our employees. We expect a candidate to take direction but also work without direction once fully trained. A candidate that had a lot of autonomy in a past job is ideal, but not necessary. This is another opportunity to see if the candidate will talk trash a former employer or boss.

6. **Why are you leaving your present job?** I don't really care about the reason. I'm looking for the candidate to finally break down and talk trash. People can hide who they are for quite a long time, but given enough time talking they will revert to their true selves. This is another reason you let the candidate do 90% of the talking—you

want to make sure by the end of the interview they have revealed their true self.

7. **What is important to you in the company you work for?** This is another two-purpose question. First, will they talk trash here directly or indirectly about a previous employer? Are you seeing a theme? We are looking for rude behavior. Second, this question lets us collect data on what employees are looking for so we can become a preferred employer among employees. It's a two-way street after all. You are being interviewed as well.
8. **What kind of person do you find it most difficult to work with and why?** You guessed it—will they talk trash or just speak in generalities? Also, I want to know how they handle dealing with difficult people. As hard as it might be to believe, guests can sometimes be difficult.
9. **What is one thing you would like to avoid in a job and why?** If the candidate has not started talking trash by now you might have a winner. The answer to this question also helps us to become a preferred employer. We have modified demotivating policies, like cellphone use during a shift, from the information we gleaned from questions like this.
10. **What might make you leave this job?** As I said, a bad attitude is a fatal sin. I don't want to hire any whiners, slackers, or pigs. They can ruin your reputation in an instant. Pigs are what we call rude employees. I'm also looking for a pending future obligation that has yet to be revealed, like a planned move or certification in a different field.

Pro Tip Revisited: Did you know more people are killed by pigs than sharks? More businesses are killed by the pigs they hire than by the shark competitors trying to steal market share. Avoid or set free the pigs and the sharks become irrelevant.

Mic drop.

11. **What is one thing your friends would say about you?** Friends can be brutally honest. Your candidate is thoroughly warmed up by now. They just might say something incriminating, like "He'll be late to his own funeral."
12. **What one thing irritates you about other people and how do you deal with it?** Would you believe me if I told you this is the last question we ask to test for rudeness? We are serious about our reputation and so should you be. Don't hire pigs and set free any pigs currently in your employ.

*Pro Tip Revisited: The best way to know you've made a hiring mistake is to ask yourself this one question, **"Would I hire this person if they came in today looking for a job?"** If no, set the ~~pig~~ employee free. You'll both be grateful.*

13. **Under what circumstances do you think work policies should NOT be followed?** Assuming you have no illegal work policies the answer should be, "There are no

circumstances when work policies should not be followed." Your policies should be tried and tested by now. If not, you'll enjoy the chapter on that subject. I'm looking for two things here: if the candidate has violated work policy in the past did they do it because they felt it was in the best interest of the company (usually also the best interest of the customer) and that they understand we like our work policies and expect them to follow them.

There you have it. **Hire for attitude** and communicate anything you think might be untasteful but is a necessary part of getting your job done. The former is for your benefit and the latter is so the candidate can bail early before either of you have spent time, money, and energy in a working relationship.

What's Next?

- ✓ Use the formal interview to test for attitude; you probably can teach them all the skills they need to know for your job.
- ✓ Be sure to communicate anything untasteful about the job you are offering to scare away anyone who might waste your time, money, and energy by quitting shortly after being hired because they don't like to clean, for example.

Chapter 5. Let Them Go in 5 Days

The Proven Policy That Saves Your Online Reputation, Keeps Your Superstars from Leaving and Saves Thousands of Dollars

Have you ever dated the wrong person? You likely dated that person longer than either of you wished. What if you had set that person free after the first five dates?

You probably knew it wasn't going to work out after the first date. Wouldn't it have saved you money, heartache, and time? Exactly.

That's why I propose adopting a **five-workday probation period** for all new employees. You will **save money** on training, it's the most ethical thing to do, and you can get back to work immediately finding the right employee.

***Pro Tip:** Firing an employee is stressful for both employee and employer. Make the process more positive and productive by changing your attitude. Instead of firing employees, think of it as setting them free— free to find employment more suited for their skills and temperament.*

How to Identify a Wrong Hire

There are two unforgivable sins in my businesses:

1. You are rude to the guests.
2. You are unable or unwilling to clean.

These two sins are unforgivable because **you cannot train for attitude** and cleanliness is vital in the service industry.

You must decide what is important to you. Here are some of the most common reasons to set them free in five days, or anytime: performance, attitude, insubordination, harassment, attendance, and safety violations. No matter the cause be sure to set them free properly and respectfully.

---

*Pro Tip: The best way to know you've made a hiring mistake is to ask yourself this one question, **"Would I hire this person if they came in today looking for a job?"** In fact, I request managers ask this question frequently regarding their entire team. If the answer is "No, I would not hire this person," then answer the question, "Why wouldn't I hire this person?" That will be the reason you should set them free.*

In three decades of hiring employees, **my companies have always paid the lowest unemployment insurance rates** available because they follow a consistently applied progressive discipline policy.

The employee knows company policies and standards, receives an oral reprimand for violations, receives a written reprimand, and then termination. The progression can be accelerated for certain violations like criminal, discriminatory, or harassment behaviors, for example, but such accelerated discipline must be clearly identified in your employee manual.

If you adopt a five-day probation period, you can still use a progressive discipline policy and it is highly recommended. Always follow the laws for your jurisdiction.

5 Reasons to Fire New Hires in 5 Days

Set Them Free before They Damage Your Online Reputation

For example, a Cornell Hospitality Report titled, Hotel Performance Impact of Socially Engaging with Consumers (Anderson, 2016), re-confirmed an earlier study that **hotel revenue is directly associated with TripAdvisor ratings**. Better ratings equal increased revenues. Don't wait until you get the disparaging reviews.

Set Them Free before They Cost You Thousands in Training

Hiring a new employee **costs an average of $4,129 to $7,645.** For example, the 2019 U.S. Bureau of Labor Statistics estimates an annualized employee **turnover rate of 45.00%** across all industries. If you operate an 11-person staff, a 45.00% turnover rate will **cost you between $20,645 to $38,225 each year**. Set them free in five days before you spend thousands on training an unworthy employee.

Set Them Free before They Cause Your Superstars to Leave

You probably already know that employees quit because of a bad boss. It's generally considered one of the top reasons employees leave. In the same vein, **employees leave when they are required to work with rude, unproductive, or bullying employees**. Set the unworthy employee free in five days to keep your superstar employees from leaving.

Set Them Free Before It Becomes Problematic to Set Them Free

There are many ways terminating an employee can become problematic. Unemployment insurance liability may not go into effect until a certain number of days of employment. For example, in Illinois, an employer is not chargeable until the thirtieth day of employment. That means if you terminate the employee and they make an unemployment-insurance claim you can deny your chargeability based on the 30-day rule.

The longer the employee works the harder it can be to terminate an employee due to misplaced compassion and weak bench strength. Set them free in five days to avoid complications of time.

Is It Legal & Ethical to Set Them Free in Five Days?

Consult legal counsel in your jurisdiction to determine if this is legal, but in most cases, if you are not violating discrimination laws, it is legal.

Is it ethical? Let's recognize that not all jobs are for all people. Hospitality jobs, for example, are especially rigorous. The hours, the guests, and the work are all demanding. **It takes a special person**.

Also, if the job is not a fit, **neither the employee nor the employer is happy**. Why should you or the employee prolong the dissatisfaction longer than five days? What is the point of waiting the 30, 60, or 90 days of the traditional probation periods?

You know they don't fit. They know they don't fit. **It is a kindness to set them free** to seek satisfying employment elsewhere.

Pro Tip: Implement a progressive discipline process for employee behavior issues and to inform the employee there is a performance problem and an opportunity for improvement. Typical steps include:

Verbal Counseling: Counsel the employee about a behavior issue and the company policy violated with a warning that continued inappropriate behavior may result in termination.

This step is delivered verbally but you must document this discussion in the employee's written record—date, time, and what was discussed.

Some policies, like theft and safety violations, might trigger immediate termination if stated in the employee policy manual.

Written Reprimand: *Discuss a twice repeated offense and document in a written form. The employee gets a copy.*

Termination Reprimand: *Deliver a final written reprimand for a thrice-repeated offense. The employee gets a copy.*

Why Do Managers Hang on to Dead Weight?

There are two main reasons.

First, they don't have any bench strength—no one waiting to fill that position. The solution is to be in a constant state of hiring. **When a superstar walks in your door you better hire them—available position or not.** Put their start date two weeks into the future. You'll have an opening by then, I promise.

Second, the manager feels it's an **act of compassion** to give the recruit a million chances. **How's that working for you?** Set the trainee free in five days and take control of your position vacancies instead of frantically trying to fill holes left when they quit without notice.

In Summary…

You maximize your staff's productivity by setting free an incompetent employee the first week.

First, your trainer can either get back to normal duties or start training a worthy candidate. The quicker you bring on the next candidate, the faster you can have a productive employee on the crew.

Second, your top performers won't have to work with an incompetent employee for the next 90 days before you decide to terminate their employment, or they find another job and leave. **Top performers will be dissatisfied working with slackers**. You'll lose your superstars over time if you don't give them competent people to assist with the workload.

This sounds crazy on the surface—fire your new employee in five days if they are not a fit. It's going to increase your turnover rate—unless you don't include these false starts in your data. You could call these first five days a paid working interview if you have heartburn with high turnover rates.

Let's face the facts, **employees are not sticking around no matter what you do**. You will see a dramatic decline in real turnover. The new employees that survive the first five days will stay longer and **your top performers will be ecstatic** that you are giving them productive co-workers who have their back.

Set the unworthy new hires free in five days and everyone will be glad you did.

Finally, you'll drastically reduce the number of whiners, slackers, and people with too many personal obligations in your workforce. This will save you time, money, and headache later.

What's Next?

- ✓ Consider a five-day probation period to save money, time, and energy.
- ✓ Change your mindset from firing to setting free—free to find employment more suited for their skills and temperament.
- ✓ Set new hires free quickly so your superstars don't leave because they don't want to work with slackers and pigs.
- ✓ Set new hires free quickly so they don't ruin your online and community reputations.

Chapter 6. Onboarding That Gets Employees Productive Quickly

Why Small Business Must Onboard Quickly to Keep from Overwhelming Their Superstars

Big companies use sophisticated software, cute onboarding gifts, and boring orientation sessions to onboard their employees. **Small business does not have the luxury to be so wasteful** and that's a good thing.

Productive onboarding is important, however. Part-time employees productively onboarded will **stay longer**, **understand what is most important**, and **become profitable** for the business faster. After all, you don't hire employees for their benefit, you hire them for the benefit of the business. You need them to make money fast.

Productive Onboarding Can…

1. **Engage employees** when they are most excited to work for you. If your new hire is not asking questions they are disengaged already and might be unmotivated. You cannot train for laziness. However, you are responsible for creating an environment where the new hires feel comfortable to ask questions. Have you made it clear that you expect them to ask questions throughout the

onboarding process? Do you answer questions in a meaningful way that makes the new hire feel like they not only understand the "how" but also the "why?" Employees who understand why are more likely to follow the "how"—i.e., do the job exactly the way you want it done.

2. **Set expectations** now so there are fewer misunderstandings later. You already know half the battle is won when you clearly communicate expectations. Did you know you win the entire battle when you add a "because" to every expectation communicated? We expect you to sanitize the counter because we don't want to spread disease through surface contact. We expect you to recognize every guest as they walk through the door because it makes the guest feel special and then they are not annoyed about waiting to be served. We expect you to show up to work five minutes early because your fellow employees would like to end their shift on time.

3. **Get the employee up to speed fast** so they make a return on your investment sooner rather than later. Obvious, I know, right? So why do so many small businesses take so damn long to get their new hires onboarded? Get the fluff out of your onboarding process. Here is a shortlist of where to find fluff in your onboarding process:
    a. Required reading (Unfortunately for us the State health department makes our staff read War and Peace–length Regulations. Nothing can disengage an employee faster than boring as hell regulations. Break up the reading into chunks.)

    b. Forms (Are all the forms necessary? Have someone on hand to answer questions so the new hire is not stymied and frustrated filling out your forms.)
    c. Orientation (Do you like the sound of your voice? No long introduction speeches.)
    d. Introductions (Cut the small talk down to, "Welcome to the team, we are excited you are here.")
    e. Facility Tours (Don't get bogged down at the water cooler.)

Where big businesses often take up to 90 days to get a new employee integrated and onboard, we take a mere five days. Yep, **new part-time hires are onboard in five days or they are overboard**. Most of the time we know the first couple of days if a new hire is a fit with our values and culture.

Here is our onboarding plan developed over years of trial and error. Incorporate what you like into your onboarding plan.

General Onboarding Guidelines

1. **Onboarding can be boring**; make sure to mix up the boring stuff with the fun stuff. It all must be learned; it doesn't all have to be learned in a specific order.
2. **Everyone participates** in a new part-time employee onboarding, but most of the training is done by a manager to help maintain consistency. When you have a deep bench of superstars, who does the training becomes less important.
3. **It's a race** to get the new employee onboarded in five days. Keep and maintain the momentum so we get the

employee productive quickly and so we waste little time, money, and energy on training someone who might not pass muster.

4. **The trainee is responsible for their training.** Our new hires fully understand they have five days to onboard. They must have their five-page training checklist with them at every shift. They must nag, if necessary, the veterans to train them. We've found this shift of responsibility, from the company to the new hire, is key to getting the training done in five days. It also identifies new hires that lack self-motivation—laziness and rudeness are two character traits you can't change.

5. At any time during these five days, if we determine the new hire is unwilling or unable to clean or is rude **we immediately set them free** (using a consistent procedure for all new hires) to find work more suited for their skills and temperament. It's a kindness to the new hire and it's a superstar retention tactic. Your superstars do not want to work with whiners, slackers, and pigs.

Onboarding Checklist We Use

Before Day One

1. **Get the new hire's workstation and equipment needs ready.** Don't make the new hire hunt down what they need to do their job. I worked with a nursing home that hired a bookkeeper but had no computer for her to use. Unless you are still using paper books (God help you) your bookkeeper needs a computer.
2. **Pre-frame the new hire to your staff.** When you get your staff excited about the new hire, they will be more

receptive and have high expectations. You can pre-frame this way, "The new guy starts tomorrow" or this way, "Please be sure to welcome the newest member of our team tomorrow. She's a bright college student studying finance at the university. You're going to love her positive nature." The latter pre-frames the new hire in a way that sets her up for success.

3. **Send a welcome email** to reinforce the new hire's decision to work for you. You might say something like this, "Welcome to the XYZ family. You've made the right decision to join the XYZ family and here are the reasons why: (list benefits here)." You have now pre-framed the company in the mind of the new hire. They are expecting a positive experience.

Pro Tip: *Include parking instructions in the welcome email. It's the little things that make life easier, don't you think?*

---

4. **Include all the necessary paperwork in advance** (immigration, income tax, non-disclosure agreements, non-compete agreements) so there is less time wasted on day one.
5. **Many of our part-timers have never filled out a government form.** We highlight all the fields on the immigration and income tax withholding forms so there is less confusion about what information is required. Also, we make it clear we need to see their identification documents as required on the government form instructions.

6. Have you used an email drip campaign to market to your customers? Try using an **email drip campaign to onboard your new hires**. Drips are easier to drink than the traditional firehose used to convey important information.
    a. Email 1: Welcome email with paperwork attached, confirm email did not end up in a spam folder
    b. Emails 2–6: Training material for Days One through Five
    c. Emails 7 and beyond: Important policies highlight, policy changes, special guest promotions

Day One

1. Orientation
2. Tour: Location of The Open Sign, Lights, Drop & Employee Safes, Mop Sink, Bucket, Mop, Cleaning Supplies, Toiletries
3. Expectations
4. Required Reading (boring, yawn…)
5. The Perfect Sunless Tan
6. Everyone Is Responsible for Sales and Everything Supports Making Sales

Day Two

1. Guest Room Preparation
2. If You Have Free Time to Lean You Have Free Time to Clean
3. Sales Training

Day Three & Four

1. Salon Cleaning (Did I mention how important cleaning is?)
2. Sunless Booth Cleaning
3. Restroom Cleaning
4. Sales Training

Day Five

1. Finish Any Missing Checklist Items
2. Sales Training
3. Successful Completion of Bed Runner Exam
4. Evaluation by District Manager
    a. Review Bed Runner Exam Results
    b. Demonstrates Interest in Using Our Products and Services
    c. Demonstrates A Positive Attitude and A Willingness to Learn

You must determine what information to communicate during the onboarding: industry-specific, company values, and operational tactics. They should know how to use the tools of your trade, dress code, scheduling, payday, and all the other specifics. **Productive onboarding means your new hire stays for the long haul, understands your expectations, and is ready to hit the proverbial ground running—fast.**

What's Next?

- ✓ **It's a race**—onboard fast so your superstars can be productive again.

- ✓ **Set expectations early** so there is no confusion about responsibilities.
- ✓ Use a **new-employee email drip campaign** to facilitate the onboarding.

Chapter 7. Deliver Smart Evaluations That Make Superstars Want to Stay

Why Recognition Is the Most Valuable Benefit a Small Business Can Offer

Truth be told I hate giving formal evaluations. I hated receiving them as well. I was a nervous wreck for each one I received. About 20 years ago I decided to ask my staff how effective they felt these formal annual evaluations were. They told me they hate them and that they are a nervous wreck for each.

We stopped doing annual formal evaluations—they are especially worthless for part-time staff.

What is far more effective is Ken Blanchard (Blanchard, 1982) and Spencer Johnson's approach to **setting goals** (expectations), **reprimanding behavior**, and **praising individuals** (evaluations) as they lay it out in their book *The One Minute Manager*.

In a nutshell when you make your expectations (setting goals) crystal clear, no doubt in anyone's mind, this is the way we want it done, by when, and here's why, no one is surprised when they are reprimanded or praised for their behavior.

If you wait a year, a quarter, a month, or even a week to praise or reprimand behavior you've already missed the chance for either the praise or reprimand to be effective. And you've allowed mistakes to fester which cost you tens of thousands in real money and reputation.

Additionally, giving an attagirl or attaboy when the behavior occurs is the cheapest high-value benefit you can offer your part-time staff. Your staff is recognition starved—feed them often and they will be superstars.

Genuine Praise (Recognition) Is a Cheap High-Value Employee Benefit

I love giving praise. Nothing lights up my face like seeing the facial expression of a person I have just praised. You should try it.

Here are the rules for giving praise:

1. **Make it genuine.** False praise is to your staff what ass-kissing is to you. When you attempt to catch people doing things right, you'll have no shortage of real praise to give.
2. **Make it public** if you can. Unlike a reprimand, which is always done in private, praise is amplified when it is given in public—especially in front of a customer.
3. **Make it immediately**. People do what they are consistently rewarded for doing. The longer you wait to give the praise, the less positive reinforcing effect it has. Additionally, you don't want your staff to ever feel like you take them for granted. Good work unrecognized makes you look unappreciative and ungrateful. This is where employee resentment grows.

There you have it: Make it genuine, make it public, and make it immediately. Half the recipe for effective evaluations is to make a million praises all year long. Make it your job number one to seek out and catch your employees doing things right.

Short Reprimand of Behavior

There are two main purposes of a reprimand: to correct behavior and to document repeated violations of policy. I wouldn't bother with the latter if it weren't necessary to prove cause for terminating an employee. Just like praising, there are rules for giving reprimands:

1. Target the behavior and never the individual—behavior bad, person good.
2. Keep it private. A reprimand done in public is called a shaming and is not constructive in correcting behavior. A reprimand done in front of a customer is called a lost customer. Don't do it.
3. Make it quick. Deliver the reprimand as close as possible to when the behavior occurred and spend less than one minute delivering the reprimand.
4. Make it constructive. Describe the offense and the policy it violates: "You were late for work which violates the Timeliness policy." Explain why you have this policy: "When you are late for work it means your fellow employees have to pick up the slack. They might need to leave work on time for a doctor's appointment, for example. The customer is underserved when we are understaffed. That could cost us customers which is where we get revenue to pay salaries for all the employees." Ask the employee what they are going to do

so they are not late to work again. Let them know what repeated violation of the policy means, like possible termination.
5. Leave them feeling valued. Remind them you value them and their work, but you have higher expectations of them. And then let them return to work. The whole thing should take less than one minute.
6. Document the reprimand in the employee's permanent file. Especially oral reprimands must be documented as you will not remember the who, what, where, why, and how of the behavior.
7. And finally, forgive and forget about it. Do not hold a grudge. Do not stew over the incident. You'll die young of a heart attack.

Forget the annual evaluations. Use a million micro evaluations all year long, both praising and reprimand varieties, to get the most out of your people so they can perform like superstars. **Your part-time staff will stay for the long haul because you've paid them lavishly in praise and recognition**.

What's Next?

- ✓ Make expectations (goals) crystal clear—this is the way we want you to do it, by when, and here's why, so no one is surprised when they are reprimanded or praised for their behavior.
- ✓ Give immediate genuine praise a million times a year by catching your staff doing things right.
- ✓ Quickly and privately reprimand undesirable behavior—attack the behavior, not the individual.

Chapter 8. Engaging Employees with Meaningful and Diverse Work

Things That Make You Say, "That's Obvious."

Employee engagement is all the rage.

As a small business owner reading the latest and greatest about engaging employees, I find myself, well, disengaging from the business gurus.

Here is the list of words from one consultant's website who sells employee engagement surveys (I think): performance, strategic, alignment, competency, satisfaction, benchmarked, engagement, survey, intentional, bridge, execute, challenges, empowers, respects, confidence, factors, culture, motivation, relationships, cohesive, accountable, expectations, organization, communication, and **my favorite phrase, multi-directional communication strategy.**

My eyes are glazing over.

I'm reluctant to write on this topic because if you do everything else right employee engagement is the natural byproduct. My ex-wife would tell me, **"That is obvious, why are you even mentioning this to me?"**

In fact, I'm apologizing in advance for such a short chapter on the topic. The one piece of advice I have is important, it just isn't that difficult or complicated. **And I gave away the secret in the heading.**

Engage your employees by giving them meaningful and diverse work. You don't like doing boring things and you sure as hell don't want to do the same thing day in and day out. That's why I work for myself: meaningful and diverse work. Have your employees try your job or part of it. Cross-train positions—they'll be excited to learn something new and, wait for it, you'll have a backup for that position.

Now, go walk in your employee's shoes and if you are bored to tears, mix it up a bit for them.

That's it. We're done here.

Next…

What's Next?

- ✓ Assign some of your more interesting duties to your staff so they feel engaged and valued. The worst that can happen is you have less work to do.
- ✓ Cross-train staff to keep things interesting, fresh, and engaging. Your superstars will stay for the long haul and you'll have a backup for all your positions.

Chapter 9. Retire Demotivating Policies So Your Superstars Can Excel

In the Absence of Rules, People Make Up Their Own Rules

Have you noticed how raw you feel **when the opposing team cheats**—when they play by a different set of rules? That's when the greatest disharmony occurs. The same disharmony can happen when well-meaning people play by different rules.

Conversely, when like-minded people team up under an invisible bond, an unwritten code, great results can be achieved. The bond between soldiers in a military unit is a great example. Written policies or even laws almost become unnecessary.

This part is about **adopting a code of honor,** a set of rules that brings out the best in every person who subscribes to it. Then simultaneously, suggesting you identify and **retire demotivating policies** so your staff can be productive again.

How a Code of Honor Can Make Policy Enforcement Easier

A code of honor is best developed with the team to ensure buy-in. Otherwise, you might just be forcing values on your staff that they simply can't follow—it's not part of their character.

Once the team makes the code of honor part of the company culture, then all new hires become easier. **Hire those who match your values. Set free those who do not**.

Here is our Code of Honor every employee signs and agrees to follow upon being hired. Just in case, we include a signature line for those who don't agree to the Code of Honor and choose not to be hired. No one has ever signed the second line, but it reinforces that we are serious.

Sample Code of Honor

In the absence of rules, people make up their own rules. Some of the biggest upsets, collisions, and disharmony occur because well-meaning people are simply playing by different sets of rules. By the same token, the most miraculous results come from like-minded people who team up under an invisible bond to achieve greatness. Sometimes the easiest and best way to avoid upset, collisions, and disharmony in a team is to make sure everyone is playing by the same rules. A Code of Honor is that set of rules and brings out the best in every person who subscribes to it.

The following is our Code of Honor:

Never Abandon a Teammate in Need

Be Willing to Call and Be Called

Keep All Agreements and Clean Up Any Broken Agreement Immediately

Deal Directly with the Person You Have a Problem with or Let It Go

Be Responsible—No Laying Blame, No Justifications

Be Resourceful—Find Solutions Before Dumping on Others

Never Let Personal Matters Get in the Way of Your Mission

Be Loyal to the Team

Commit to Personal Development

Don't Seek or Ask for Sympathy or Acknowledgment

Everyone Must Sell

Celebrate Wins

___ **I accept and subscribe** *to this Code of Honor. I will uphold this Code for myself and help other team members to do the same.*

___ **I can NOT accept** *and subscribe to this Code of Honor. I hereby submit my resignation.*

The Code of Honor sets expectations. Maybe instead of doing annual employee evaluations, you whip out the employee's signed Code of Honor and review it with them. Ask them to reaffirm your Code of Honor to reset and reestablish their responsibility to the team. The right core values, or code of honor, make most policies unnecessary because the team is cohesive and plays by the same rules.

Why Your Policies Kill Productivity, Add Expense, and Drive Away Talent

> ***Reiteration of Legal Disclaimer:*** *I am not an attorney. I don't even play one on TV. This is not legal advice; you should not consider this advice without consulting your attorney.*

I hate to give you the bad news, but **your employees only agree with about 52% of your policies** based on a survey of seven different policy areas. That means 48% (Corso, 2018) of your policies have a demotivating effect on your staff.

If this were Major League Baseball, you'd be batting .520 which would make you better than Ty Cobb who is the all-time leader in career batting average at .366. In business, **missing the ball 48% of the time is losing you a lot of employees, money, and productivity**.

You cannot train for a lazy unmotivated character trait. You can momentarily motivate an individual with a carrot or a stick. However, you cannot maintain a state of perpetual motivation in another person through your training or policies. **You can completely and wholly demotivate your staff with bad policies**.

You must seek out those demotivating policies and purge them root and stem.

I was conducting a training on this subject when a student asked me, "**How do we know which policies are**

demotivating?" At the time I was stymied. I could give the student examples, but I didn't have a definitive way to identify them until now.

I gathered all the demotivating policies we changed or retired and came up with these common denominators:

1. **The policy is unenforceable**. Remember Prohibition? It was a colossal failure. The law was created because the supporters believed alcohol was the root of almost all of society's problems. Alcohol consumption did go down but crime, especially violent crime, went up. **We had a "no cell phone" policy**. I know, funny right? We were spending all our reprimand capital writing up employees for violating the "no cell phone" policy. And what was worse, we allowed managers to have cell phones because on occasion the salon landline phones would be left off the hook and we needed a way to communicate with the salons. The solution was a policy that outlined the appropriate use of a personal cell phone during a work shift. Everyone was happier.
2. **The policy is frequently being waived**. If you find yourself constantly allowing staff to ignore a policy, then you should consider retiring it or modifying it. We had a policy that staff could not use the salon's services (free to staff as a perk) outside of business hours. We found ourselves granting exemptions because of scheduling conflicts to avoid making the staff upset about not getting to use one of their benefits.
3. **The policy makes the job harder**. I sometimes call this the 5% policy. You create a policy because if you didn't 5% of your staff or customers would be jerks and take

advantage of your good graces. We used to have the policy of attaching a digital photo of every guest to their account. This was to prevent guests from sharing memberships. The problem is that the process adds time and hassle to signing up the member, guests do not come to us camera-ready (sometimes they arrive in pajamas), so they are salty about getting a picture taken, and when we are too busy, staff would not take the picture anyway. We decided to drop the policy and accept the handful of jerks who will take advantage of our good graces. We are much happier as a result.

Today, not tomorrow, analyze your existing policies for demotivating potential. I'm sorry, but 48% of your policies have the potential to demotivate. When you seek you shall find bad policies. Retire or change them before they cost you more money and talent.

While you are conducting this company self-awareness analysis, get your team together to figure out what your core values are. Once you have consensus, codify those values into a Code of Honor that gets the whole team playing with the same set of rules to create harmony. **Your superstars will stay for the long haul and be productive again which will improve your bottom line.**

What's Next?

- ✓ Create harmony by getting consensus on company core values and then codify them into a Code of Honor.
- ✓ Seek out demotivating policies and retire or change them so your superstars can be productive again.

- ✓ Instead of annual evaluations, consider an annual reaffirmation of your Code of Honor.

Chapter 10. What's Next?

Massive Imperfect Action Leads to Success

Use the three-minute screening interview in conjunction with accurate interviews, short probationary periods, productive onboarding, effective evaluations, meaningful & diverse work, and common-sense policies to recruit, hire, and retain superstar employees. You'll drastically reduce the number of slackers and people with too many personal obligations who make it to the interview process and into your workforce. This will save you time, money, and headache later.

If this sounds daunting, book a free consult with me to transform your workforce into productive, cohesive, team-players who stay for the long haul, and contribute to innovation and excellence on the job (and could really benefit your bottom line).

Your To-Do Checklist

- ✓ Job postings must describe the person, not the position, both what you want and don't want. Include this line in every job posting to filter out what you don't want: **No whiners. No lazy people. Nobody with too many "personal commitments."**

- ✓ Evaluate your existing staff against these criteria so you know where to make room on your bus for a superstar: **"Would I hire this person if they walked through the door today?"**
- ✓ Become a preferred employer so superstars come knocking on your door.
    - o **Don't be an asshole!** Assholes repel potential superstars and chase away existing superstars.
    - o **Gently poach superstars** in your community by giving them something more valuable than money and in short supply—**recognition**.
    - o **Fix broken promises quickly.** No one is perfect and no one expects you to be. When you screw up, admit it, apologize, and make it right—fast!
- ✓ **Hire fast and fire quick**—hiring should be more like speed dating.
- ✓ Pre-qualify part-time employee candidates with a **three-minute telephone interview** so you can drastically reduce the number of slackers who make it to the formal interview process and into your workforce.
- ✓ Consider a **five-day probation period** to save money, time, and energy.
- ✓ Change your **mindset from firing to setting free** —free to find employment more suited for their skills and temperament.
- ✓ Set unworthy new hires free quickly so your superstars don't leave because they don't want to work with slackers and pigs.
- ✓ Set unworthy new hires free quickly so they don't ruin your online and community reputations.

- ✓ It's a race—**onboard fast** so your superstars can be productive again.
- ✓ **Set expectations early** so there is no confusion about responsibilities.
- ✓ Use a **new-employee email drip campaign** to facilitate the onboarding.
- ✓ **Make expectations (goals) crystal clear**—this is the way we want you to do it, by when, and here's why, so no one is surprised when they are reprimanded or praised for their behavior.
- ✓ **Give immediate genuine praise** a million times a year by catching your staff doing things right.
- ✓ **Quickly and privately reprimand** undesirable behavior—attack the behavior, not the individual.
- ✓ Assign some of your **more interesting duties to your staff so they feel engaged and valued**. The worst that can happen is you have less work to do.
- ✓ **Cross-train staff** to keep things interesting, fresh, and engaging. Your superstars will stay for the long haul and you'll have a backup for all your positions.
- ✓ **Create harmony** by getting consensus on company core values and then codify them into a Code of Honor.
- ✓ Seek out demotivating policies and retire or change them so your superstars can be productive again.
- ✓ Instead of annual evaluations, consider an annual **reaffirmation of your Code of Honor**.

References

Anderson, C. &. (2016). *Hotel Performance Impact of Socially Engaging with Consumers.* Cornell SC Johson College of Business. Ithaca: The Hotel School.

Blanchard, K. P. (1982). *The One Minute Manager.* New York: William Morrow & Co., Inc.

Collins, J. (2001). *Good To Great: Why Some Companies Make The Leap and Others Don't.* New York: Harper-Collins Publishers.

Corso, J. (2018). *The Definitive Guide to Employee Onboarding.* San Francisco: YourPeople, Inc.

Glassdoor Team. (2019, July 5). *How To Calculate Cost Per-Hire.* Retrieved from Glassdoor for Employers: https://www.glassdoor.com/employers/blog/calculate-cost-per-hire/

Meiner, D. (2015, June 1). *What Do Personality Tests Really Reveal?* Retrieved from Society of Human Resource Management Web Site: https://www.shrm.org/hr-today/news/hr-magazine/pages/0615-personality-tests.aspx

Myers, T. R. (2018, May 10). *Why our facial expressions don't reflect our feelings.* Retrieved from BBC Future Web Site: https://www.bbc.com/future/article/20180510-why-our-facial-expressions-dont-reflect-our-feelings

Northon, L. &. (2016, August 3). *2016 Human Capital Benchmarking Report.* Retrieved from Society for Human Resource Management: https://www.shrm.org/about-shrm/press-room/press-releases/pages/human-capital-benchmarking-report.aspx

Sherman, J. E. (2018, June 29). *Universal Qualities of Jerks.* Retrieved from Psychology Today Web Site: https://www.psychologytoday.com/us/blog/ambigamy/201806/universal-qualities-jerks

U.S. Bureau of Labor Statistics. (2020, March 17). *Economic News Release.* Retrieved from U.S. Bureau of Labor Statistics Web Site: https://www.bls.gov/news.release/jolts.t16.htm

About the Author

Don Kermath

I've been self-employed since I was old enough to hold a leaf rake, a snow shovel, and a bottle of Windex. You could say I got the entrepreneurial bug early.

I've had employees since 1988—and never laid off one due to mismanagement or lack of work. I have, however, set free (aka fired) my share of whiners, slackers, and pigs.

I'm still standing after all these years. I'm still running a business—doing, not just teaching. Oh, and I run my businesses from 714 miles away. That's because I learned how to run my businesses and not have them run me—which they did for many years.

I have something to offer you can't learn in business school. Life and business failures have taught me a valuable lesson—everything is impermanent. That includes success as well as failure. When you accept impermanence you live your life and run your business gratefully and mindfully.

It's a happier existence.

If this sounds daunting, book a free consult with me to transform your workforce into productive, cohesive, team-players who stay for the long haul, and contribute to innovation and excellence on the job (and could really benefit your bottom line).

Find out more at https://www.DonKermath.com

Can I Ask a Favor?

If you enjoyed this book, found it useful, or otherwise then I'd really appreciate it if you would post a short review on Amazon. I especially would love to hear what you loved about the book. I do read all the reviews personally so that I can continually write what people are wanting.

If you'd like to leave a review then please visit the book page and leave a review:

   www.amazon.com/dp/B08PB1C7JV

Thanks for your support!

Winning the Recession

Get your copy today of this Amazon #1 New Release. *Winning the Recession* is a small business action guide to remaining profitable during a recession.

A few businesses will thrive during a recession and increase profits while most will see profits decline. However, if you want to win the recession, you must take actionable steps now.

This Action Guide is designed to help you win the recession and remain profitable. There is no reason your business can't win the recession. Here is how to take advantage of opportunities during a recession.

www.amazon.com/dp/B0BS73SBGW

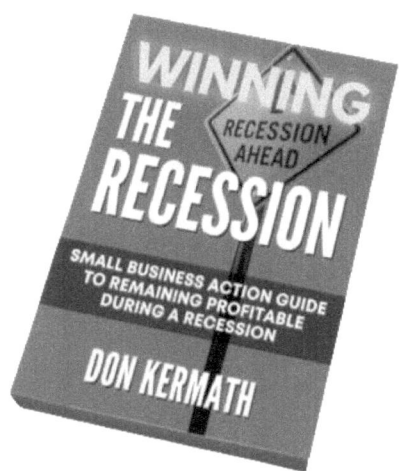

Here's what you'll learn:

- How recessions affect small businesses
- **The 10 exact winning revenue opportunities available during a recession**
- Why now is the time to raise your prices
- **The 14 hidden winning expense-cutting opportunities at your disposal anytime**
- Why you should clarify your competitive advantage during a recession
- **Where to find the gold mine you didn't know you already have**
- The 11 winning pro tips to be profitable during a recession

www.ingramcontent.com/pod-product-compliance
Lightning Source LLC
Chambersburg PA
CBHW030449220526
45464CB00006B/2457